Soulful Whispers

Lyrics from Soul

Dr Radha Gaur

BookLeaf Publishing

India | USA | UK

Made with ❤ on the BookLeaf Publishing Platform
www.bookleafpub.in
www.bookleafpub.com

Dedication

To my husband, my best friend, my greatest supporter. My children who continue to inspire me with their narratives.The teachers who appreciated my ability to think critically. My Parents who taught me values, I could never shrug off. The people who joined me in my journey and taught me some valuable lessons.

Preface

It gives me immense pleasure to present "Soulful
 Whispers", a panorama of emotional
recollections of events, memories and episodes from day
to day life. I sincerely hope that each poem resonates in
the minds of the readers and makes an enjoyable
reading.

Dr Radha Gaur

Acknowledgements

I would like to thank Book Leaf Publishing for giving me opportunity to express myself and presenting the verses from my soul before the readers.
I would also like to thank Dr Neha Jain whose constant persuations motivated me to get my work published.

A Farewell to Bygones

Ups and down, past and future
are just phases of life,
One will come, come and go,
Just take them in your stride.

Unpleasant past like a spear
shall make us cry,
But forget the tears and the pain
Let bygones just go by.

Let past be a lesson
to tread a glorious path,
With new hopes and passion
and forget the woeful wrath.

If some unpleasant memories
remind you of the dark,
see the golden sunshine
and move on with a spark.

Do not let your souls be slaves,
to the hurdles of the past,
Arise, aspire, desire and dream
remember this is not the last.

If you want to succeed,
You will have to flow,
On the wings of hope and grit
Like the glowworm glows.

Forget the past and move ahead
With your head held high,
Let mind be free of gloom
And lips of a sigh!

Epoch: A Flight of Time

As I grow older,
I push the heavy cart;
Priceless are the memories
Locked away in heart.

They tag along like shadows,
Wherever I go;
Like the little saplings,
Planted in a row.
Harbinging a smile or tear
whenever i sit and plough.

The glee of carefree childhood
Floats before my eyes;
As the steps move forward
The rougish innocence dies.

The toil and the labour
As you fend for life;
Some mirth and songs of laughter
And the endless strife.

The journey and the people,
who made it all along;

Cascading joy's and sorrows,
As one by one they throng.

Memories make you richer
As you sit and think;
Hush! do enjoy the panorama
and let the feelings sink.

Perception Matters

Few eyes peeped out of door ajar,
Some saw mud and some stars.
This is right or that is true;
They thought and thought and then withdrew.

For some, the bounties are half empty,
For some, the glass is half full,
Some lament for "what is not"
Others enjoy bounties to the full.

Bushes and shrubs scare some eyes,
And some stare at greens galore.
So it is not the eyes that see,
But what the mind is looking for.

Deep waters are rhe rouges for some,
Dumb founding are desert mirage;
We look at things as we want to see,
Or some deep emotions are at large.

Who saw what and what he saw?
Do not let the confusion grow,
One saw mud and others saw stars,
it was reality they both saw.

In Melody and Rain

When fingers play on strings of heart,
Just hold my hand and sing.

When flowers bloom and rain drops fall,
Just hold my hand and sing.

Lost in the melody of humming birds,
Just hold my hand and sing.

When playful waves make me dance,
Just hold my hand and sing.

When my quivering lips beckon you,
Just hold my hand and sing.

When I fumble and look back,
Just hold my hand and sing.

The ups and downs shall wear me down,
Just hold my hand and sing.

When moist eyes shed a drop,
Just hold my hand and sing.

Pristine Delight

Years after, in lap of nature,
I sat on window sill;
It was a lazy morn,
And everything was still.

The infant rays at dawn,
Were spreading golden hue,
Like an eager bride,
Waiting for her beau.

Old buddies, the tall palms;
Whispered, while they swayed,
The gentle breeze forced them apart
And they pleasantly were dismayed.

The yellow winged butterfly,
On dew capped rose alights
Flapping wings in rhythm,
Tired from her flights.

The sluggish sun, like a bride
from behind the hills doth peep,
A little drizzle broke the spell
And made the squirrels squeak.

Jolted from my haze
I jerked upright;
Encompassing was nature,
In all it's glorious might.

Our chores keep us busy
In the mundane life,
And what all we are missing
In success, as we stride.

The Inner Demons

She surged and swayed,
To let something unfold;
She rose like a phantom,
As if to revolt.

I sat there in silence,
A little bit surprised,
My notions and emotions,
Very well surmised.

The blue and white waves,
With calm ripples flow;
Embittered though sometimes,
They their resentment show.

Alas! like us fretting mortals,
They want to break the flow;
The deep hidden turmoil
They also want to show.

There are many barriers
Which do not let one speak;
Memories, duties, obligations
And many promises to keep.

These waves are just to share
What havoc is in mind,
To express, unfurl our hidden tsunamis
Thus, hail triumphant from our grind.

Halt and lend a helping hand,
To those unfurling their minds;
One shall be like the ethereal waves
While helping thus mankind!

The Snap Shot

For oft, my eyes fell upon this snapshot,
It seems ages before it was shot;
Ample faces, beaming with cheerful joy
As children, every bit we enjoy.

Getting up early with half closed eyes,
Some angry whining and stiffled cries;
In jiffy we were off to school
To study, play and oft to fool.

How often we planted coins in ground,
So that they yield money abound.
Our names were writ on a pole till end
With all our shares and dividends.

What fun it was, no worries and care,
Multiple stories for each to share.
New games created by genius minds
Tips were shared from few behind.

We laughed, fought and played the pranks,
In parks, trees and on river banks.
So soon we grew and parted ways,
With lingering scents of carefree days.

For oft alone I sat and wept,
This cherished treasure, I have kept,
In my childhood, to let me dive,
And let that innocence in me thrive.

New frames though fill the house abound,
Keep childhood friends always around,
Their jokes, keep the childhood in you alive,
To fight with odds and survive.

Lessons in Disguise

My disillusioned self, lacked thanks giving,
And I always cursed my life ;
why lesser minds had more than merit
And failures in my stride?

But i feel, I am blessed
and God's favourite child,
He dragged me up a tough terrain ,
while I sat and riled.

Mishaps in life, made me strong
And brought to fore my fortitude;
In hopelessness, I could walk alone,
My greatest gift was solitude.

My pain taught me to walk alone
With smile and head held high;
My failures taught me not to brood,
Just get up try and try.

My struggles taught me humility,
And grit to bravely steer,
Holding on when waves are rough,
With mettle instead of fear.

With folded hands I thank you Lord
For wisdom through this pain;
I prayed to shine, you gave me lusture,
Your efforts have not gone invain.

Alluring Nature

The flowers bloom, the birds chirp,
And sun spreads it's golden glow;
The trees sway to the whistling winds,
Not ready to bow.

Velvet hillsides akin cascading waters
Are so proud of their home,
Quaking ducks and shoal of fish,
Enjoying the wavy foam.

Unfurling petals, kissing dew drops
Is a site to behold;
So many mysteries hidden behind,
Eager to unfold.

The innocent fawn, squels in delight,
Lurking somewhere behind;
The squeaks and chatter are in tune,
As if to unwind.

So much to see and learn,
From the beauty here abound,
Carefree joy and rhythmic frolic
In harmony all around.

Sit down in the lap of nature,
And let magic unfold,
So many marvels, so many sagas
Buried here untold.

Truth: Unsung Virtue

"Truth" though preached, marches in solitude
And often lags in pace.
"Lies " are deceivers, much adored,
And often earn the praise.
Some truth are harsh and face the ire,
lies are flatterers; soft and warm,
which we often admire.

Some truths earn wrath and dislike
And hardships in its life,
Lies deceive, Yet adored by all,
Is a feather in its pride.
"Undaunting Truths" roar is loud,
but often shuts the door.
"Lies", a graceful enchantress.
Wins, accolades as it soars.

Lies have got a golden sheen,
Which charms all when spoken,
Truth is often kicked aside,
So better left unspoken.

Clasping Thee to my Heart

Clasping thee to my heart, I see
Beauty in weary life,
Your zest for life, give me wings
From mundane woes to flee.

Your words are like a soothing balm
Which often cure my aches;
Those half closed eyes and lurking smile ,
are harbingers of calm.

Clasping thee to my heart, i forget ,
How timid i can be;
A novel hope, a gusty twinkle ,
New courage I beget.

Clasping thee to my heart, I set out
To explore the riddles unknown.
With you by my side to hold my hand,
Yonder are the days, I dream about.

Clasping thee to my heart, in bliss
I spend my days,
As hand in hand, we row the boat,

I seal this with a kiss.

19

Ego; The Manipulator

Ego is devious friend,
That does more harm than good;
Slowly it follows the heart,
For years where it stood.

Ego is sly,
And plays a dangerous game;
It make us more pompous,
With every leap in fame.

It Slowly engulfs and entwines,
And we bid farewell to truth,
One by one they all depart,
Dear buddies from our youth.

Ego goads and taunts us,
And we learn to boast,
Name, fame and power,
We want at any cost.

Beware! do not be selfish
And don't confuse with pride;
With fame nurture humility,
Let gratitude in heart abide.

Crestfallen Hope

Hope, like a falcon
Travels swiftly on its wings;
It stealthily alights in our hearts
And sometimes it stings.

It cluthches mankind
Like a creeper entwined;
It loosens it's hold,
Leaping miseries untold.

Hope is a deceiver,
It flatters the heart;
And charms thine eyes,
With astonishing arts.

Like a pretty maiden,
With enchanting smile laden;
It embalms our foolish minds
Then vanishes leaving us shaken.

It is truth for you to discover,
Once bitten by hope, you cannot recover.
It burns bright and flashes
But later it ends in ashes.

The Black Box

One afternoon at leisure,
I opened the long forgotten black box;
For many years it lay in the corner,
Housing so many treasures.

It was long since I opened it,
A prize which was so dear,
Many things are left behind
Like seasons advance in year.

The tattered doll, my mother's gift,
A tiny frock, a pair of shoes and a little bow,
Some toys, some games and some frames
Forgotten as we grow.

The pen was gifted by my father
While explaining of its might;
When confused and at crossroads,
Do always what is right.

Some torn books, my soul mates,
From the years that went by,
My wedding gown had lost its sheen
Oh, how soon the time flies.

This box, like kaleidoscope,
Many fables doth unfold;
Enthralled, I laugh at memories,
Which are never old.

Untamed I walk

What is this fear, that invades my mind,
It grips me, terrifies me with words unkind.
What is this fear, I do not know.
Should I explore or withdraw.

Is it the ruptured trust, some unkind notes,
or agony of past hurt, or betrayal floats.
Can it he the lengthy nights alone,
Memories of friends, long lost or gone.

Is it the fear of being left alone,
or is it the emptiness syndrome?
How to move on and take the risk,
My trembling legs can't walk so brisk.

A fear of speaking, lest be misunderstood,
Tired of giving as much as you could;
To match the pace with changing landscapes,
Some unknown fear takes irrational shapes.

Fear shall not dim my spark,
Unheeded on new voyage I embark;
To get rid of fear, I shall find a way,
so unrestrained, untamed, I walk away.

Simple Joys; A pure Bliss

No time to pause, no time to breathe,
The more you get, the more you need.
Ranting about frivolous vows,
In mimicking others, confusion grows.

The laughter echoes when someone mocks,
Giggles arise at silly jokes.
Simple life and it's joys are lost,
No more gather to raise the toast.

Comrades occupied, hardly call;
whistling kettle unheard in hall.
Empty are the parks, where kids had fun,
No more chattering dames under the sun.

Small little Joy's, yield no pleasure,
Mundane days; for lack of leisure,
Let us all decrease our pace,
Enjoy while you are part of this race.

Feel the bliss in small errands,
Have some coffee with your friends,
Nurture relations with love and care,
Don't be swayed by frivolous glare.

Adversity

As I slog on the edge,
with darkness all around;
On gravelled path, are prickly thorns,
And no encouraging sounds.

The steeper does my climb becomes,
More so my courage wanes;
The "Right" path is not always smooth
With no incentives or gains.

Then a "Voice "whispers to my shattered soul;
"You have managed well so far;
unflinching faith that you kept,
is worth every scar".

"Easy gains by shrewd and crafty,
May break you everyday;
Priceless wisdom is your gain
While scaling this taxing way."

"You were frail, I gave obstacles
To gift you fortitude;
kindness, compassion and empathy
Along with humble attitude."

"All those glitter are not gold;
I wanted you to see.
Your gratitude and unflinching faith,
Have brought you closer to Me."

Friendship Amidst Chaos

Trying to board a moving train,
One hand pulled me inside;
You want to live or die instead,
"You think and than decide."

I looked up and saw,
Two lips parted in a grin,
He gave a chuckle and smile,
Though eyes seemed little grim.

I was horrified to see
Things strewn all around;
He swiftly moved to clean the mess
That irritated me profound.

We sat silently for minutes few,
He soon began to speak,
From where he comes and where he goes
As if an explanation was due.

His innocence slowly won my heart,
And I began to tell;
of failures and struggling years.
My pain I could not quell.

We differed in our thoughts and manners,
But somehow our dreams aligned.
Something somewhere struck a chord,
A friendship was destined.

So many years have gone by,
Our friendship has that spark
Fond memories of our meeting,
To gossips in the park.

Two of us were tossed along by Some,
In this cosmos so vast;
as if to script a friendship,
Destined to last.

A Tribute

Fondly remembering my teachers,
With folded hand and gratitude;
I remember those guiding hands,
Who pruned the path, I chose to tread.
And held my hands at all the bends

They gave me a canvas to paint,
My aspirations and thoughts so bright;
They punctuated my wild logic,
With stories of truth and toil.
Often they had no answers to my inner turmoil.
Yet they could sow the seeds,
Of virtue and honest intent.

No words can ever pay the debt,
Nor my gratitude show.
But I now nurture young saplings,
Carefully in a row.
I paint canvas with some dreams,
For these young minds to see;
In this way I share the gift,
once given to me.

Life: A Paradox

There was a juncture,
when life for me had a different picture;
It was for me a rosy dream,
Like ducks, I waded in this scented stream.

My toys, my school, my books,
Picnics and truants with the crooks,
Unending gossips under the shady trees,
The fun and frolic at studies.
That was the golden phase I must say,
Can such memories be erased; nay

As in age, I began to grow,
A different inference i had to draw.
Years began to loose their superficial flow
I saw the deep hidden pitch below
It is not just beauty, that we call life,
But misery, vowes and endless strife.

Here mean may rise and greatness fall
Wounds struck deep by the hands of a pal,
Where mortals are ground by the stone;
till they are crushed to the very bone.

What turn it takes, I do not know.
But do we reap as we sow??
Are the helping hands rushed,
to soothe the writhing masses crushed.

Has the merit its own reward,
Is not timid by bold often cawed.
Don't on lies and greed some dwell,
Even when they hear the knell.
So in life the meanings change,
And lot depends on our visions range.

A Love that Lasts

Those innocent eyes, tugged my soul,
And my heart skipped a beat;
It was love I know now,
Though, then it was discreet.

Few syllables said to each other,
could make us understand;
We weaved love, with threads of trust,
As we danced hand in hand.

You stood firm in my despair,
And never left my side;
with gentle care and gallant love,
I swam across the tide.

Laughter echoed in our hearth and home,
And cherished moments shared.
Hand in hand we faced the tides,
All ups and downs fared.

Heart entwined in love divine,
All tears and joy's we face,
Me applauding all your strengths,
My frailty you embrace.

With each day passing,
There is surplus of mutual love and care;
No secrets kept in this kinship,
Faith and trust we share.

Moments sealed in fun and gaiety,
With love and care in hearts;
This is the love, that wades through odds,
This is the love that lasts.

www.ingramcontent.com/pod-product-compliance
Lightning Source LLC
Chambersburg PA
CBHW071233140726
47996CB00007B/2585